VIA Folios 71

HARVEST

HARVEST

poems by
EMANUEL DI PASQUALE

BORDIGHERA PRESS

Library of Congress Control Number: 2011913424

©2011 by Emanuel di Pasquale.

All rights reserved. Parts of this book may be reprinted only by written permission from the authors, and may not be reproduced for publication in book, magazine, or electronic media of any kind, except in quotations for purposes of literary reviews by critics.

Printed in the United States.

Published by
BORDIGHERA PRESS
John D. Calandra Italian American Institute
25 W. 43rd Street, 17th Floor
New York, NY 10036

VIA Folios 71
ISBN 978–1–59954–028–3

PUBLISHED POEMS

"Sicilian Mask"
The Sewanee Review

"Long Branch, Late August Windy-Wintry Day"
The Alhambra 2009 Calendar

"Death"
The New York Quarterly

"Aurora, God's Wings"
The New York Quarterly

"Caught off the Metuchen, New Jersey, Train Station Wall"
The New York Quarterly

"For My Father"
The Journal of New Jersey Poets

"Do Not Fear"
Lips

"On the Occasion of a CHELSEA Reading . . ."
The Journal of New Jersey Poets

Contents

Harvest • 11

Stir • 12

True Love • 13

On the Occasion of a Chelsea Poetry Reading
at 5th Avenue Between 42nd and 43rd Street • 14

In Long Branch, this August 10th • 16

Sicilian Mask: • 17

May Wind-Storm in Long Branch • 19

Father's Day, 2007 • 20

"Blessed be purple bird shit" • 21

And Then • 22

Genesis • 23

Equality? • 24

ancient mountain burials • 25

Deep into the Lagoon • 26

When You • 27

Father/Mother • 28

"The snake that knows neither rust nor hurry" • 29

Mango • 30

Long Branch, Late August Windy-Wintry Day • 31

Ebb and Flow • 32

Death Comes • 33

For My Father • 34

Letter from My Cousin, Vacationing in Spain • 35

A Student's Lament • 36

On the Musical Score of the Film, *Jeremiah Johnson* • 37

I Hear the Wind's Been Looking for Me • 38

Early Fall, East Brunswick's Pond by the Public Library • 39

Rain • 40

A Certain Kind of Death • 41

Aurora, God's Wings • 42

Do Not Fear • 43

Caught Off the Metuchen, New Jersey Train Station Wall • 44

A Word of Advice • 45

Death • 46

Buried • 47

The Hudson River • 48

Northeaster • 49

No More • 50

The Dead • 51

God Is • 52

Maya • 53

About the Poet • 55

Harvest

In early August, the first berries
Have burst black (small grape clusters)
Along the Jersey shore
Here in the high dunes of Long Branch
I harvest a bunch—some thirty
Ripe ones after the thick rain

"How are the berries?" asks a walker
From the boardwalk. "Juicy, a few."
"Good," he answers and walks on.

The next walker grimaces,
His wife holds him back by the arm.
"Are they safe to eat?"
I reach up, hand him a few. He puts one in his mouth.
Spits it out.
His wife pulls him away.

At dawn, I'll harvest the next batch
The night will ripen.

STIR

The sun burns
Through a fir tree

Rises
Dries clouds
Dust

Longing for song
Washes over blue jay

Spins scythe
Of land sand
Into gold

The red hills fall
Into the lake
And the long-legged heron
Pauses

True Love

Insane Love that heals
As a sepulcher heals flesh:
Eats it,
Rots it,
Consumes marrow, blood,
Transmutes it into carbon,
Into sugar flakes.

ON THE OCCASION OF A CHELSEA POETRY READING AT 5TH AVENUE BETWEEN 42ND AND 43RD STREET

Lost within her unfocused eyes
A blue-eyed child
Two buttons missing from her frayed leather shirt,
Blonde, escorted by a many-ringed woman

By Seward's statue
At the base
A man wrapped in woolen caps and scarves
Sleeps lost in the marble

At Starbucks Union Square, crochet and macramé,
Soft-faced, companionable Marion, one of the vendors,
Guides me through the waiting line.
"You're after me," she says. How small the espresso for two bucks—
Two, three sips. How thin its flavor.
At the park, the water pulsates in the granite fountain.
And George Washington's right hand, extended,
As it has been for 150 years,
Leads a reluctant horse,
Head curved, nostrils flaring

Gandhi, bamboo stick in hand, keeps on smiling.
An untouched mackintosh by his right toe.
He doesn't mind the dried-up carnations staining his bronze toga,

Heavy wings for any angelic flight.
The holy mother holds her baby by the red swings,
And a Kobricks coffee deliverer beeps for her to 'cross already'

Later, Tim Liu and Marilyn Hacker read from a chair at Fifth Avenue for Chelsea.
From down the street, the two stone lions strain to hear.

In Long Branch, this August 10th

The trees on South Beach and Ocean Blvd
Are in love with the winds

All day into twilight
And night now
What tossing of hair
What loosening of braids
From pine maple oak—
What laughter from the long grass
And white and red prairie rose
What dizzying laughter
From the long and lean white lampposts—
All overwhelms today
All winds and wings

Sicilian Mask:

> *How can you trust this man?*
> *Look, he has the mask of Sicily on his face.*
> —The Godfather, Part II

The face of the monster on the mountain
The monster on Mount Ibla

Rock walls separate farm fields
The face of the farmer on each stone
Twisted by sweat, sand.
The gloved fist of France
And Spain

The monster on the church façade
Face of cretin
Chains, knives, stiletto heels
Hidden torture chamber below the main
Altars of churches. Carmelites, Assunzione, Immaculate Conception,
Saint John the Baptist red rooster crown head on a plate blood
Saint Rosalia licking Palermo plague-free
The hammer and the sickle;

HARVEST

Quasimodo trekking up to Rome,
Poems in his back pocket,
His father's face sketched deeply on the palm of his hand
(he closes it, holds it like a treasure)

Quasimodo, like a lily,
Like a red rose
Like a yellow rose
Like a white rose

The mask of Sicily on his face

EMANUEL DI PASQUALE

May Wind-Storm in Long Branch

A few large white-grey gulls
Four or five
Fly low over the ocean
Through the waves
Rise like planes
Then give into the air

Two sparrows, small bullets,
Shoot out, south

The boardwalk's cedar planks are half dry
Licked by the wind's dry tongue

The young, flowerless tulip
Bends its thin branches
And the long leaves dance and sing:
It is all joy
In the thundering ocean

Father's Day, 2007

It's snowing blossoms in Long Branch
In the high winds of ocean
Dandelion puffs carve the air—
Sperm and ovum driven

(but for the perfectly cut grass,
A crew-cut, well-behaved),
It is all Life

But birds are driven to sing
Endlessly, this morning,
And children dig holes in the skies
With their brown eyes

Lovers dare not unglue themselves
From each other: the suck and slurp,
The murmur, the prayer

Today, God lives in the high winds
And human sweat . . .

Blessed be purple bird shit
On my balcony
Blessed be Bach
Blessed be spring blossoms
The white, the red dogwood
Blessed be icicles in wintry ocean
In Long Branch along South Bath Avenue
Blessed be the bushes of mulberries, white and black,
Along the shore
Blessed be earth worms
Lost on cement walkways
After a storm
Blessed be mating butterflies
And old women sucking cigarettes
On a frozen lake in Vestal, New York
Blessed be my hand
Shaping these words
Blessed be the Word
And blessed be vinegar and salt

And Then
for Emily Dickinson

You're a thunderstorm
Antideluvian
Swollen river sea
And then a dew
A lake on a maple leaf

Genesis

The stars,
The unusual stars,
The stars that wanted to be, to see—
The large-eyed stars
That wanted to be seen

The emptiness that wanted to be filled,
That wanted to fill—
The stars
The dust that dreamed,
That spun itself into being—
The stars

Equality?

And that's always been Her story—
Banned for biting the apple,
For wanting to know

Branded dirty, impure for giving birth

Only vestal virgins go to heaven, not the mother of any Jesus

Boys hunt them down like wingless she-birds
Then blame for being caught in nets

Let the blood flow on dusty floors

(and let death follow)

ANCIENT MOUNTAIN BURIALS
for John Keats

Masons cracked them open
For eternal reasons
In Ibla, Sicily,
Half way from the Rotonda
To the cemetery
And down into a riverless valley
Burial sheet
Bone
Blood
And flesh
Eaten by silence and time

Along the marble hills
Single burying cells
Small rectangles, squares
(empty eye sockets)
No bone survives
No ancient coin
No queenly necklace
No simple scratch to mark a name

Nothing survives
But empty eye sockets

Rock eggs

Deep into the Lagoon

Giant crabs will take years
To rip a whole whale's body
Clean into pure bone

When You

When you began to turn the key
To open the door into tenderness and love,
I was here by the sea, waiting in the patience
Of wave and wind to find a mate
Whose open eyes advised of her open soul.
There is no fear in your eyes,
Fierce and soft as purple petals
There is no fear in your flesh.
Come then and be my ocean
Even as I am your ocean.

Father/Mother

Sun, father, life-spinner, light-giver
Steady murderer

We come from nothing—physics, calculus, from
Alchemy and slime—from blind science

Oh mother how can we find you?

What Voice Speaks? "In the ocean,
In your blood: salt driven,
In your tears. In April, when the bud
Leafs green."

The snake that knows neither rust nor hurry
Lowers its head and slowly slips into the belly of earth
Small lakes spin into black sleep
And large rocks lie thoughtful
Till clear-eyed lovers wake the waters
And in a world born over
Stir the swallow and the butterfly.
Horses run in the wide mornings of farm fields.
The limbs push of trees spills into branches
And buds and into leaves that leak like tongues.

Mango

Mango, my daughter's hamster,
Digs her nasty toes, rips my blue shirt.
"She hangs on," my daughter smiles.

Long Branch, Late August Windy-Wintry Day
for X J Kennedy

When Frank Mullen's sons moved him
And his wife, Gerry, from their ocean home
To a park trailer in Freehold,
Frank looked at me, his mother-of-pearl
Eyeballs swimming in decades of beer and swill,
Lowered his head, and peeped, "Emanuel,
I will see you in heaven." And I sensed my own fate,
And saw it clearly today, in the pre-wintry chill
Of arrow northern rain—a couple blocks
From my ocean view: maroon torn
Annnunciation—West End Manor—Motel Style
Bdrm available. From its windowless rooms,
Non Si vedono le stelle. Otherwise, all is well.

Ebb and Flow

There is no return
There is no reason to return
But we for a long time
Don't know it
Such a long time
There is no return
But once we know it
In our blood
In our brain
After much love
After much hurt
After the tear of children:
The wide eyes
Full moon white
Spine cell
After much hurt
After much love
Then each of us becomes our own brother
Each of us becomes our own sister
Each of us becomes our own father
Our own mother
And we freely take the long breath
And we become ocean,
Ebb and flow

Death Comes

Death comes like a mother
Like a woman holding her child
Be the fireplace
While the snow gathers heft
Tests the roof
As it packs into ice

Loose sparks find dry cracks,
Devour the house
And the flames embrace us,
Transmute us into cinders,
Into spires of fire,
And fly us home.

For My Father

My father's coffin was no cedar—
It was the poor man's burying wood:
A few planks of uneven oak,
Old Fig. and so his essence melted,
Mixing into the earth around his long rectangle—
And when his ten years of public burial
Came around, and he was dug out,
Skin still stuck to his bones,
Eyes to sockets, hair to skull—
Even his grey striped suit kept faith—
And his thin tongue still sang—
So said the grave keeper.

Letter from My Cousin, Vacationing in Spain

I swam in the Atlantic and didn't see you,
Emanuel. I looked for you over the Azores,
Called your name: sea gulls screeched.
I imagined you in Long Branch,
By South Bath Avenue, sensed you
Body-surfing tall, rooster-waves.

    Summer's end
    Early September

The ocean welcomes warm human flesh
For one more month in the northern sphere.

Come
Come

    Swim in the mother waters of lower
Mediterranean
    All year round.

A Student's Lament

Five thousand years and thousands of gods,
Murder, incest, and nothing has changed.
We must accept mortality.
Be tight with our morality.
Be Enkidu or Patroklus
And die and pave the way
For haughty Gilgamesh or Achilles.
So much to read.
When all I want is wine
And the weed
Thousands of words
That I try to read
But stay mere words
I cannot even breathe
Let alone read
Thank god for pot
And wine

On the Musical Score of the Film, *Jeremiah Johnson*

There is no musical score in real life,
Only the scare of snow—
A silent doe, prancing, aiming to be shot,
Blue firs mirroring our loneliness
Insanity of women without men
Children huddling in the corners of rooms
And the angels struggling in a frozen river
And the blind moon faking light
Black moon spinning loon
Black rock moon fake white goon

I Hear the Wind's Been Looking for Me

I hear the wind's been looking for me
It roared overhead
And curled the waves
And tried to spell my name (Eman Eman Eman)
After all its howling
Circled by my balcony and
Excited birds to sing "Emanuel"
And finally after my long silence
Had them pause on wires over my Toyota
I found an E, red from strawberries
And a purple d, from blueberries
On the windshield
And now that I'm home
It's gone
Leaving mist and dew
All over Long Branch,
More ocean bits

Early Fall, East Brunswick's Pond by the Public Library
for Steven Barnhart

The world of god metes out its sweet boredom
Not one tree is untouched by Fall
Bunches of leaves surrounded by brown halo
Small squirrels sniff and scratch soaked woodchips
The aerator shoots out
Three climbing waterfalls
So carp can keep on living
Geese work their wide wings
Croak and run across the pond
Signs for Peace, scarves,
Embrace a young birch
Next to a marble monument
For boys and girls lost to the last war

Inside the library
Sleek fans
Drones pinned to the ceiling
Scatter cool air

Measured click clock of heels
Of old woman ambling
To the latte counter
Fast flip flap of children
Rushing to computers
An aged man forming poetry
On two pink scraps of paper

Rain

The peace that rain brings
Over sand by ocean
Over leaves of forest
Over wings of sea gull
Redbreast
Rain that fills puddles with tadpoles
That fattens worms into monarch butterflies

A Certain Kind of Death

The horror of the tail cut off
From the warrior horse
From the pit bull
The horror of any Dragon
Submitting to saint George
The horror of the Erect Snake
Crawling on its belly
Losing its supple limbs
Its wide wings

Aurora, God's Wings

Does Black-Borealis come from light?
Does it have its own life?
Is death the back hand of life, or the palm?
Is sleep small death or life-driving, driven?
Eagles that mate in the high skies
And orgasm as they fall?
Does life blossom from the fall of death?
The burst of black that yearned to be seen, to see?

Do Not Fear

Do not fear
Do not fear dust nor dusk:
Do not fear clouds nor the gathering of clouds
Do not fear the blackness of tunnels
Do not fear for rain follows dust and darkness
Rain as drizzle pine needles arrows rains as monuments:
Buds plants trees. Always rain
Always brightness and song
Washing into salt into the ocean of blood

Caught Off the Metuchen, New Jersey Train Station Wall

I do not love you,
Isolyna Rivera
No more forever

A Word of Advice

Among you there is
one who feels the heat of
stars in his veins,
one who knows the worm
as his brother, the starfish
as his sister; among you
there is one that prays
to the moving waters
of brooks, rivulets,
and rivers, one who whistles
the song of blue jay and cardinal, one
for whom the starling
returns year after
year; among you
there is one for whom babies smile and to
whom young children
run to, one
whose living eye
spooks the rabbi
and priest, one who
feasts at the joys of love.
Isolate him—quickly—
tear his guts open,
stone him,
drown him—
protect our dun limbs
from his glow.
Then go on your usual ways.

Death

Blue death shines like a halo over the dead dog;
It leaves him to sleep in too much peace,
And rushes into streams and the tops of trees.

Buried

We should be buried in forests,
In mountains, like leaves fallen into deep cracks,
The origins of brooks,
Rivers, rivulets

We should be buried far from the seas
And let the rains, our fathers,
Carry us in their fluid arms back home,
Into the mothers' spinning waves

THE HUDSON RIVER

Thick ropes, the waters of the Hudson
Tie me up, bind me, roll me from Albany
Down to New York City—
Like a free-falling log
Held in the current's tight hold.

EMANUEL DI PASQUALE

NORTHEASTER

Northeaster rips along the boardwalk
Strewing white petals
From the prairie rose

No More

No more lesser light
Washing the ocean white

No more noonday flood

No more rain
Swelling grass green

No more nights made wild
By your bird song

Oh my child

The Dead

They wave at us
Old ladies leaning against companionable birches
Little girls in long white dresses
Men bent over like aged flowers
They wave at us
From a small island
In the middle of a lake so calm
Only the sun's reflecting gold betrays water
Hands waving
              Slowly
"We are here
Waiting
We are here"

God Is
for R. W. Emerson

Slate flakes into sand and dust

The robin sings

Waterfalls trill

Blue ocean currents curl red and white

Thighs open to thighs

A child looks open-eyed

Clouds weep to rain

Dirt and sunlight split open
The asparagus' head

Toes bend

Spine-bone churns blood cells

And Whitman gathers
Under my boot sole

Maya

The diviners make one mistake after another
They can't cure my restlessness
At least the earth gives you potatoes
If the rains come
If the sun radiates

I know the spirit is in the body, is in the body
Perhaps a photograph can capture it
An X-ray for sure

Somewhere where balls and brain meet
In that liquidity that connects and heals

Oh, Pegasus, strike that rock hard,
Shatter it.

About the Poet

EMANUEL DI PASQUALE was born in Ragusa, Sicily, and emigrated to America in 1957. He earned a Master of Arts from New York University in 1966. Since then, he has taught college English.

His translations from the Italian include *Sharing a Trip*, by Silvio Ramat (2000); *Infinite Present*, co-translated with Michael Palma (2001); *The Journey Ends Here*, by Carlo della Corte; and *Between the Blast Furnaces and the Dizzyness*, by Milo De Angelis. His poetry books in English include *Genesis* (1989), *The Silver Lake Love Poems* (2000), *Escapes the Night* (2001), *Carthweel to the Moon* (2003), and *Writing Anew: New and Selected Poems* (2007). Sections of his book *Genesis* were translated into Italian by Carmela Muscarà (with an introduction by Giovanni Occhipinti) with the title *Un'ambra prigioniera* (2002).

Di Pasquale has received the following awards: Bordighera Poetry Prize for translating Joe Salerno's *Song of the Tulip Tree* into Italian (1998); Academy of American Poets' Raiziss/de Palchi Fellowship for translating Silvio Ramat's *Sharing a Trip* into English (2000); Chelsea Poetry Award for *Connections: Prose Poems of Rome, Sicily, and Venice* (2002); and a National Italian American Foundation grant for translating contemporary Italian poets into English (2002).

He lives in front of the Atlantic Ocean with his daughter, Elisabeth Raffaela.

VIA FOLIOS
A refereed book series dedicated to the culture of Italian Americans in North America.

HELEN BAROLINI, *Crossing the Alps*, Vol. 65, Fiction, $14
COSMO FERRARA, *Profiles of Italian Americans*, Vol. 64, Italian American Studies, $16
GIL FAGIANI, *Chianti in Connecticut*, Vol. 63, Poetry, $10
PIERO BASSETTI AND NICCOLÓ D'AQUINO, *Italic Lessons*, Vol. 62, Ital. Amer. Studies, $10
G. CAVALIERI & S. PASCARELLI, eds., *The Poet's Cookbook*, Vol. 61, Recipes/Poetry, $12
EMANUEL DI PASQUALE, *Siciliana*, Vol. 60, Poetry, $8
NATALIA COSTA-ZALESSOW, ed., *Bufalini*, Vol. 59, Poetry, $18
RICHARD VETERE, *Baroque*, Vol. 58, Fiction, $18
LEWIS TURCO, *La Famiglia/The Family*, Vol. 57, Memoir, $15
NICK JAMES MILETI, *The Unscrupulous*, Vol. 56, Humanities, $20
BASSETTI, ACCOLLA, D'AQUINO, *Italici: An Encounter with Piero Bassetti*, Vol. 55, Ital. Studies, $8
GIOSE FIMANELLI, *The Three-legged One*, Vol. 54, Fiction, $15
CHARLES KLOPP, *Bele Antiche Stòrie*, Vol. 53, Criticism, $25
JOSEPH RICAPITO, *Second Wave*, Vol. 52, Poetry, $12
GARY MORMINO, *Italians in Florida*, Vol. 51, History, $15
GIANFRANCO ANGELUCCI, *Federico F.*, Vol. 50, Fiction, $15
ANTHONY VALERIO, *The Little Sailor*, Vol. 49, Memoir, $9
ROSS TALARICO, *The Reptilian Interludes*, Vol. 48, Poetry, $15
RACHEL GUIDO DEVRIES, *Teeny Tiny Tino's Fishing Story*, Vol. 47, Children's Literature, $6
EMANUEL DI PASQUALE, *Writing Anew*, Vol. 46, Poetry, $15
MARIA FAMÀ, *Looking for Cover*, Vol. 45, Poetry, $12
ANTHONY VALERIO, *Toni Cade Bambara's One Sicilian Night*, Vol. 44, Poetry, $10
EMANUEL CARNEVALI, Dennis Barone, ed., *Furnished Rooms*, Vol. 43, Poetry, $14
BRENT ADKINS, ET AL., eds., *Shifting Borders, Negotiating Places*, Vol. 42, Proceedings, $18
GEORGE GUIDA, *Low Italian*, Vol. 41, Poetry, $11
GARDDAPHÉ, GIORDANO, AND TAMBURRI, *Introducing Italian Americana*, Vol. 40, Italian American Studies, $10
DANIELA GIOSEFFI, *Blood Autumn/Autunno di sangue*, Vol. 39, Poetry, $15/$25
FRED MISURELLA, *Lies to Live by*, Vol. 38, Stories, $15
STEVEN BELLUSCIO, *Constructing a Bibliography*, Vol. 37, Italian Americana, $15
ANTHONY J. TAMBURRI, ed., *Italian Cultural Studies 2002*, Vol. 36, Essays, $18
BEA TUSIANI, *con amore*, Vol. 35, Memoir, $19
FLAVIA BRIZIO-SKOV, ed., *Reconstructing Societies in the Aftermath of War*, Vol. 34, History, $30
TAMBURRI, ET AL, eds., *Italian Cultural Studies 2001*, Vol. 33, Essays, $18
ELIZABETH G. MESSINA, ed., *In Our Own Voices*, Vol. 32, Italian American Studies, $25
STANISLAO G. PUGLIESE, *Desperate Inscriptions*, Vol. 31, History, $12
HOSTERT & TAMBURRI, eds., *Screening Ethnicity*, Vol. 30, Italian American Culture, $25

VIA FOLIOS
A refereed book series dedicated to the culture of Italian Americans in North America.

G. PARATI & B. LAWTON, eds., *Italian Cultural Studies,* Vol. 29, Essays, $18

HELEN BAROLINI, *More Italian Hours,* Vol. 28, Fiction, $16

FRANCO NASI, ed., *Intorno alla Via Emilia,* Vol. 27, Culture, $16

ARTHUR L. CLEMENTS, *The Book of Madness & Love,* Vol. 26, Poetry, $10

JOHN CASEY, ET AL., *Imagining Humanity,* Vol. 25, Interdisciplinary Studies, $18

ROBERT LIMA, *Sardinia/Sardegna,* Vol. 24, Poetry, $10

DANIELA GIOSEFFI, *Going On,* Vol. 23, Poetry, $10

ROSS TALARICO, *The Journey Home,* Vol. 22, Poetry, $12

EMANUEL DI PASQUALE, *The Silver Lake Love Poems,* Vol. 21, Poetry, $7

JOSEPH TUSIANI, *Ethnicity,* Vol. 20, Poetry, $12

JENNIFER LAGIER, *Second-Class Citizen,* Vol. 19, Poetry, $8

FELIX STEFANILE, *The Country of Absence,* Vol. 18, Poetry, $9

PHILIP CANNISTRARO, *Blackshirts,* Vol. 17, History, $12

LUIGI RUSTICHELLI, ed., *Seminario sul racconto,* Vol. 16, Narrative, $10

LEWIS TURCO, *Shaking the Family Tree,* Vol. 15, Memoirs, $9

LUIGI RUSTICHELLI, ed., *Seminario sulla drammaturgia,* Vol. 14, Theater/Essays, $10

FRED GARDAPHÈ, *Moustache Pete Is Dead! Long Live Moustache Pete!* Vol. 13, Oral Lit., $10

JONE GAILLARD CORSI, *Il libretto d'autore, 1860–1930,* Vol. 12, Criticism, $17

HELEN BAROLINI, *Chiaroscuro: Essays of Identity,* Vol. 11, Essays, $15

PICARAZZI & FEINSTEIN, eds., *An African Harlequin in Milan,* Vol. 10, Theater/Essays, $15

JOSEPH RICAPITO, *Florentine Streets & Other Poems,* Vol. 9, Poetry, $9

FRED MISURELLA, *Short Time,* Vol. 8, Novella, $7

NED CONDINI, *Quartettsatz,* Vol. 7, Poetry, $7

ANTHONY TAMBURRI, ed., *Fuori: Essays by Italian/American Lesbians and Gays,* Vol. 6, Essays, $10

ANTONIO GRAMSCI, P. Verdicchio, Trans. & Intro., *The Southern Question,* Vol. 5, SocCrit., $5

DANIELA GIOSEFFI, *Word Wounds & Water Flowers,* Vol. 4, Poetry, $8

WILEY FEINSTEIN, *Humility's Deceit: Calvino Reading Ariosto Reading Calvino,* Vol. 3, Criticism, $10

PAOLO A. GIORDANO, ed., *Joseph Tusiani: Poet, Translator, Humanist,* Vol. 2, Criticism, $25

ROBERT VISCUSI, *Oration Upon the Most Recent Death of Christopher Columbus,* Vol. 1, Poetry, $3

Published by Bordighera, Inc., an independently owned not-for-profit scholarly organization that has no legal affiliation to the University of Florida, the John D. Calandra Italian American Institute, or State University of New York at Stony Brook.

www.ingramcontent.com/pod-product-compliance
Lightning Source LLC
Chambersburg PA
CBHW072036060426
42449CB00010BA/2289